Deserts

Steve Parker

QEB Publishing

Copyright © QEB Publishing, Inc. 2008

Published in the United States by
QEB Publishing, Inc.
3 Wrigley, Suite A
Irvine, CA 92618

www.qeb-publishing.com

Library of Congress Cataloging-in-Publication Data

Parker, Steve.
   Deserts / Steve Parker.
      p. cm. -- (Planet earth)
   Includes index.
   Summary: "Describes the climate, location,
types, storms, and plants and animals of desert
ecosystems"--Provided by publisher.
   ISBN 978-1-59566-570-6
   1. Desert ecology--Juvenile literature. 2. Deserts--
Juvenile literature. I. Title.
   QH541.5.D4.P37 2009
   577.54--dc22

                    2008012612

ISBN 978 1 59566 721 2

Author Steve Parker
Design and Editorial East River Partnership

Publisher Steve Evans
Creative Director Zeta Davies

Printed and bound in China

Picture credits
(t = top, b = bottom, l = left, c = center,
FC = front cover)
Corbis 13 George H H Huey, 15 Peter Johnson,
27 Brian A Vikander

Getty Images 7t Chris Sattlberger,
8–9t Jeff Foott, 10–11 Peter Pearson,
11t Paul Chesley, 12 Karen Kasmauski,
13t Time & Life Pictures/Getty Images,
14–15t Lee Frost, 16–17 Gerd Ludwig,
20tl Michael & Patricia Fogden,
29 Bernard van Dierendonck

NHPA 20 A N T Photo Library,
21 Anthony Bannister, 21t Martin Harvey,
22–23 Martin Harvey, 22t James Carmichael Jr,
22b A N T Photo Library

Photolibrary 25t, 26–27 Gerald Hinde

Photoshot 16 Phillip Roullard

Shutterstock 1, 2, 3, 30, 31, 32 Ronen Boidek,
1 Alex James Bramwell, 1 Nelson Sirlin,
1 Dmytro Korolov, 1 pandapaw, 1 T W,
1 Johan Swanepoel, 3b Alexander Kolomietz,
4c Louise Cukrov, 4–5 Amir Hossein Biparva,
5t Alexey Goosev, 5 Vova Pomortzeff,
6–7 Stasys Eidiejus, 8 Ke Wang,
8–9b Angel's Gate Inc, 10b Kaspars Grinvalds,
12–13b Daryl Faust, 14–15b Jo Ann Snover,
16t Ashley Whitworth, 17b Ronald Sherwood,
18 Dmytro Korolov, 19b Steve Lovegrove,
19 Hagit Berkovich, 23b David Nagy,
24–25 Johan Swanepoel, 27t Johan Swanepoel,
28–29 Stephen Coburn, 30 Dhoxax, 31 Igor Karon

Words in **bold** are
explained in the glossary
on page 30.

Contents

The driest lands

Deserts can be sandy, rocky, or covered with pebbles. They can be scorching hot or freezing cold, but all deserts are dry.

People in the Gobi Desert live in tents called yurts and keep two-humped, Bactrian camels.

Wow!

The world's driest desert is the Atacama Desert in South America. In some parts, it has not rained for more than 100 years!

Dry and hot

People, animals, plants, and all other living things need water to survive. Deserts have much less water than forests or grasslands. This is because it hardly ever rains in a desert. If it does rain, the water usually dries in the hot sun, trickles through the thin soil, or flows away over bare rock. This is why many deserts appear to have so little life.

The dorcas gazelle digs for plant bulbs in the desert.

It's so... dry!

In a typical desert, if you collected all the rain that fell in a year it would amount to less than 9 inches. That is almost three times less rain than in London, England, and four times less than in New York City.

A large area of windswept sand in a desert is known as an erg.

Saving water

About one-quarter of the world's land area is either very dry or true desert. Yet even though these places are so dry, or **arid**, some plants and animals can survive here. These desert creatures and plants have special ways of saving what little water there is. Humans have lived in deserts for thousands of years, too. These people have a different way of life from those living in a town or city. You cannot simply turn on a faucet!

Where are deserts?

Most of the large deserts are found toward the middle of the world. They lie above and below the line called the equator.

Great Basin

NORTH AMERICA

Mojave

Sonoran

Chihuahua

Wow!
The Sahara Desert is about the same size as the USA, and much bigger than Australia!

Sahara

North of the equator

Many of the world's largest deserts lie north of the **equator**. One reason for this is that there is more land to the north of the equator than there is to the south. The northern deserts include the Sonoran Desert in North America, the Sahara Desert in North Africa, the Arabian Desert of the Middle East, and the Takla Makan and Gobi Deserts in Asia.

SOUTH AMERICA

Sechura

Atacama

Monte
Patagonian

It's so... big!
The Sahara Desert is four times bigger than the Arabian Desert, the world's second-largest desert. It is six times bigger than the third-largest desert, the Gobi Desert.

Largest desert

The Sahara Desert, which occupies 3,500,000 square miles, is the world's largest desert. It is about 3000 miles across. This is almost the same distance as that between London and New York.

Kara Kum

Gobi

Takla Makan

Turkestan

Thar

CHINA

Arabian

INDIA

Somali

Equator

AFRICA

South of the equator

South of the equator, both Africa and South America have deserts. These are mainly in the south-west of each **continent**. North America has deserts in its south-west, too. The place with the most deserts for its size is Australia. More than two-thirds of this huge country is dry land or desert.

Kalahari

Namib

Great Sandy

Gibson   Simpson

Great Victoria

AUSTRALIA

The largest southern dry areas are in Australia.

Antarctic

How deserts are formed

Deserts form in places where there are few rain clouds. These can be inland, along dry coasts, and in areas shielded from rain by mountains.

Around the South Pole lies frozen Antarctica. Here, it is too cold to rain.

Continental deserts

The Earth spins around once each day, so different parts are warmed by the sun at different times, and this affects where winds blow and how clouds form. Often, there are clouds and rain near sea coasts. Further inland, it is drier. The largest deserts, such as the Sahara, are far from the ocean. These are called continental deserts.

Rain falls on mountains around the Mojave Desert, not in the desert itself.

Rain-shadow deserts

Some deserts, such as the Mojave Desert in the United States, are known as rain-shadow deserts. When warm, moist air blows against mountains, it rises and becomes cooler. As it cools, the moisture in the air turns into water drops, which form clouds. As the air moves up the mountains, it loses more and more water as rain or snow. By the time the air reaches the other side of the mountains, it is dry and without clouds. Here, a rain-shadow desert forms.

Coastal deserts

Deserts are found along coasts where the winds are very dry. The Namib in south-west Africa and the Atacama in western South America are both coastal deserts.

Southern Africa's Namib Desert lies beside the cold Atlantic ocean.

Types of desert

Wow!

A strong desert wind can move a massive sand dune by 0.5 mile in a single day. Some of these sand dunes can be as large as mountains!

Many people imagine that deserts are made up of huge sand dunes. In fact, only about one-fifth of the world's desert areas are sandy.

Hard rock

The type of desert that forms depends on how much sun, wind, and rain there is, and also on the type of rock in the ground. Very hard rocks do not break easily, even when the sun makes them too hot to touch. So the desert is hard and bare.

Uluru, or Ayers Rock, is found in central Australia's desert area.

Grains of sand

Softer rocks crack as they get warm in the sun and then go cold at night. They break into small, pebble-sized lumps, then into smaller pieces, which the wind blows around. Gradually, they turn into tiny bits of rock called sand grains.

In Australia, desert rocks and pebbles are known as gibbers.

Curved sand dunes formed by desert winds are known as barchan dunes.

Sand dunes

In sandy deserts, the wind blows loose sand into hills called dunes. These dunes can take different shapes, such as waves, curves, or stars, depending on the wind's direction and speed.

It's so... hot 'n' cold!

The Gobi Desert can be 104°F by day then 14°F at night. Nowhere else is it so hot, then so cold, all in just a few hours.

Desert winds and storms

People have to wrap up well to protect themselves during desert sandstorms.

The weather in a desert is usually hot and dry, but sometimes, a huge storm can blow up. Then, almost anything can happen!

Desert storms

A storm's strong winds swirl around desert sand, forcing people and animals to take cover. Over a long period of time, these sandstorms rub and scrape rocks into strange shapes, such as arches and mushrooms. This process is called **erosion**, and the worn-off bits of rock gradually become new sand grains.

Sand blown by

Wow!

The surface of the Black Rock Desert in the United States was smooth enough for Thrust SSC to break the land-speed record with a speed of 760 miles per hour!

Supersonic car Thrust SSC breaking the land-speed record in 1997.

A flash flood hits the desert in Utah's Valley of the Gods in south-west North America.

...in desert areas can sometimes form rocky arches.

Flash floods

During a desert thunderstorm, lightning flashes, thunder booms, and rain pours down. Water surges into once-dry channels, creating an instant river. This is known as a flash flood. It washes away soil, plants, and animals. Yet in a few days, the desert is dry again. In some deserts, the drying water leaves flat, pale, glistening layers of salt. In deserts in the United States, these salt flats are called playas.

Desert plants

Plants in deserts have a difficult time. They must collect as much water as they can, cope with the scorching sun, and fight off hungry, plant-eating creatures.

Deep roots

Plants soak up water through their roots. Some desert plants have roots that go down very deep, sometimes 33 feet or more. This is as deep as five people standing on top of each other. Other plants have roots that spread out widely. This helps them take in lots of water quickly when it rains.

The saguaro cactus of south-west North America can grow to be more than 49 feet high.

Plant protection

Desert animals eat as many soft plants and leaves as they can find. This is why cacti, acacias and thornbushes have spines, prickles, or thorns. They protect these plants from being eaten.

Wow!

A side branch of the huge saguaro cactus can take more than 75 years to grow!

The welwitschia soaks up water from night-time dew.

Storing water

Some desert plants, such as the cactus, store water in their thick stems. The baobab tree of Africa holds water in its wide trunk. Other desert trees that store water include the quiver tree and Joshua tree in North America, the rare ghaf tree in the Middle East and Asia, and the gum trees of Australia.

It's so... weird!

The welwitschia of the Namib Desert is an unusual plant. It has only two leaves, which grow to be 13 feet in length and become torn and ragged. This plant lives for more than 1000 years!

Flowers in the desert

Sturt's desert pea grows in dry areas across much of Australia.

After rainfall, the desert suddenly comes alive as flowers grow quickly and make a carpet of color.

Desert flowers

Where do bright desert flowers suddenly appear from? They start as seeds that may have been lying for many years in sand, soil, or cracks in rocks. Rain makes the seeds grow, or **germinate**, into small plants whose flowers quickly open their colorful petals. Desert flowers include the orange-red desert paintbrush flower and the blood-red Sturt's desert pea.

It's so... pesky!

The North African yellow-flowered Sahara mustard plant has spread to deserts in North America. Here, it smothers all the **native** plants!

Producing seeds

When they bloom, desert flowers receive busy visitors, such as bees, flies, beetles, and butterflies. These insects hatch from eggs after the rain. They carry dust-like **pollen** from one flower to another so that flowers can make their seeds. In a few weeks, the seeds fall to the ground, where they may lie for a long time. The plants then wither and die, and the desert starts to look bare again.

Spring flowers bloom quickly in North America's Mojave Desert.

Wow!

The vansumberuu flower of the Gobi Desert is so special that people travel for days to pray to it.

Queen butterflies feed on the sweet, sticky nectar of desert flowers.

Animals of the desert

Desert animals have to take in water to survive. Yet some of them never drink!

After desert rain, insects called locusts feed on new plants, breed quickly, and form gigantic **swarms**. These swarms leave the desert and devastate many farmers' crops.

The one-humped dromedary camels of Africa and Arabia also live wild in Australia.

It's so thirsty!

A camel can go for two weeks without water. Then, in a few minutes, it can drink more than 26 gallons. This is enough water to fill a bathtub!

Dry droppings

Many desert animals are able to live solely on the water they get from eating fruits and bugs. They do not need to drink extra water. Also, these animals lose very little water from their bodies. They do not **sweat** much, produce only small amounts of **urine**, and their droppings are fairly dry.

Wandering around

Ants and termites are food for many desert creatures, including the spine-covered moloch lizard that lives in deserts in central Australia. Also known as the thorny devil, this creature wanders around slowly, snapping up ants, termites, and other bugs on its way.

With its huge ears, the fennec fox can hear the noise of bugs running over sand.

The moloch lizard is protected by its sharp spines.

Desert food

Like many desert animals, the fennec fox of the Sahara Desert eats whatever it finds. Its favorites are bugs, birds, lizards, and eggs. It will also eat fruits and berries when it finds them.

Moving in the desert

Animals that live in sandy deserts have found different ways to move around the hot, soft sand.

The North American kangaroo rat has large feet.

The marsupial mole "swims" through the sand. It comes to the surface after rainfall.

Big feet

Since small feet sink into soft sand, many desert animals have large feet. Also, these animals usually hop rather than run. The largest feet belong to the kangaroos and wallabies that live in Australian deserts. Small creatures, such as jerboas, gerbils, jirds, kangaroo rats, and hopping mice, also have big feet for their body size. They take long leaps and use their tail to keep their balance.

Wow!

Australia's marsupial mole has a pouch for its young, like a kangaroo. This pouch opens backward, otherwise it would fill with sand while it was digging!

On hot sand, lizards lift their feet in turn to cool them.

It's so agile!

The red kangaroo can jump more than 20 feet in length and 7 feet high in one massive leap.

Wriggling around

Another way that animals move about in the desert is to "swim" through sand. The sandfish of the Arabian Desert is a lizard with small legs. It wriggles into the sand to avoid the sun's heat and to find its **prey** of bugs and grubs.

Sidewinding snakes

Some desert snakes move with a motion called a "sidewind." They lift and curve their bodies sideways, leaving marks in the sand. The North American sidewinder and Namib sidewinder both do this.

A sidewinder snake forms an "S" shape as it moves over desert sand.

The camel spider has large pincers.

The desert at **night**

In the desert, one way to avoid the glaring sun and scorching heat is to sleep by day and come out at night.

Listening for danger

During the day, very few animals are seen in the desert. But at night, many creatures are active. Most of these have big eyes to see in the dark, even on the blackest night. Their big ears can hear danger and their keen noses smell food or **predators**.

Food for winter

The American desert pocket mouse comes out of its burrow at night to search for seeds and bits of plants. It takes food back to its burrow to store for the winter.

Water-holding frogs sleep underground in a slimy bag.

When the sun sets in southern Africa, the bat-eared fox comes out to hunt.

It's so... spidery!

The camel spider, which is larger than a human hand, is not a true spider. It is, in fact, an animal called a solifuge. It hunts beetles, bugs, and lizards.

Hunting at night

Most owls hunt at night, so mice and small creatures are always in danger. In North America, the cactus pygmy owl leaves its hole in a saguaro cactus to go hunting. The pharaoh eagle owl that lives in the Sahara and Arabian Desert is so big that it can catch and eat other owls!

WOW! In Australia, the barking owl does not hoot. Instead, it barks "woof, woof," just like a dog!

Burrowing owls live in underground burrows in dry areas of North and South America.

Deadly desert killers

Wow!

Only two lizards are known to have poisonous bites, and both live in American deserts. They are the Gila monster and the Mexican beaded lizard.

The desert is a dangerous place for small creatures. Big hunting animals, or predators, are ready to chase and kill them.

Cheetahs stalk, then chase prey.

Acrobatic hunters

In African deserts the world's fastest runner, the cheetah, races after prey such as hares and gazelles. The caracal, or desert lynx, of the same region is a smaller cat, but just as deadly. Amazingly, it can jump 9 feet into the air to catch flying birds.

Danger in the sky

The wedge-tailed eagle soars over dry, open country in Australia looking for prey. It does not care if the animal is alive or dead! With wings that are more than 7 feet across, it is one of the world's biggest birds of prey.

Australia's big desert lizards are called goannas.

Stings and bites

Poisonous desert animals include snakes, such as the rattlesnake of North America and the desert horned viper of Africa and Arabia. There are also poisonous spiders, such as desert tarantulas, and many kinds of scorpion with deadly tail stings.

The hyena is a powerful predator that also eats any dead animals it finds.

It's so... poisonous!

Each year, more than 100,000 people are stung by scorpions, and up to 1000 die from the poison.

Desert oasis

Deserts are not completely dry. Sometimes, there is a pond, pool, or small stream where trees grow and animals live. This is called an oasis.

Forming an oasis

Even in a desert there can be water in rocks deep under the surface. An oasis can appear where water-bearing rocks are close to the surface. Water can be sucked up by the roots of trees and bushes such as palms, tamarugos, Joshua trees, and tamarisks.

Wow!

The Okavango Delta in Africa covers about 8000 square miles, the area of New Jersey or of Wales in the UK.

Year after year, elephants remember their long route to the Okavango Delta.

It's so caring!

To fetch water, the sandgrouse flies many miles to an oasis, dips its sponge-like chest feathers into the water and flies back to its nest with a drink for its chicks.

A sandgrouse takes off after collecting water.

In Rajasthan's Great Indian Desert, water is scarce so people use it carefully.

Massive oasis

Animals travel long distances to drink and eat at an oasis. Elephant herds walk for many days through Africa's Kalahari Desert to reach the waters of the Okavango Delta in Botswana. This massive oasis, made up of pools and streams, is formed where the Okavango River flows into the surrounding dry land.

Tomorrow's desert

Deserts are under threat in many ways, including from people trying to grow crops and from the search for resources such as oil, metals, and gems.

Pumps known as "nodding donkeys" raise oil from deep underground in desert areas.

So much energy!

Hot deserts are good places to collect the sun's light or heat energy as solar power to make electricity. But solar panels disturb the wildlife and can endanger many animals.

Destroying wildlife

Some desert areas, especially in the Middle East, are dotted with oil wells that bring huge wealth. People continue to drill and dig for more oil. They also search for rocks containing precious metals and minerals, such as diamonds. Some desert areas eventually turn into vast open mines, and the wildlife is destroyed.

Turning to dust

Not all deserts are natural. In some places, deserts form when people try to grow crops in thin soil. Often, the crops fail and the soil turns to dust and blows away. This makes "new" desert areas that have no natural wildlife.

Visiting deserts

Deserts are now popular destinations for people to visit. But the big, noisy trucks these people sometimes use to get there can crush delicate desert plants and frighten shy animals.

Wow!

Bare rocky deserts are great places to look for animal fossils. The first fossil dinosaur eggs were found in the Gobi Desert in Mongolia.

Many people now visit the world's highest sand dunes in Namibia's Namib Desert.

Glossary

Arid Extremely dry, with very little rain or other forms of moisture.

Continent A large land mass, such as Africa, North America, Antarctica, and Australia.

Equator An imaginary line around the middle of the world, midway between the North Pole and South Pole.

Erosion The wearing away of soil and rocks by rain, wind, sun, sand, and ice.

Germination When a seed sends out a shoot and root and begins to grow into a plant.

Minerals A large range of natural chemical substances that make up rocks and soil.

Native A plant, animal, or person in its natural region, rather than coming from somewhere else.

Pollen Tiny, dust-like grains that must get from the male parts of a flower to the female parts so that seeds can start to form.

Predator An animal that hunts others for food.

Prey An animal that is hunted for food.

Swarm A huge gathering of creatures, usually insects such as bees, wasps, or locusts.

Sweat To give off moisture, perspiration, through the pores of the skin.

Urine The liquid waste produced by an animal.

Index